# One dark night

It's dark.
It's late.
It's raining.
All the town is sleeping.

Rob is sleeping.

Kim is sleeping.

Sue is sleeping.

Pip is sleeping.

Ben is sleeping.

Ali is sleeping.

All of Sandy Bay is asleep.

It's dark and it's late.
Jack is sleeping.

The big fat cat is sleeping, too.

4

"Woof," went Spot, "woof, woof!"
But Jack is sleeping
and Jack's fat cat is sleeping.
"Woof, woof!" went Spot.

Jack's fat cat looks up.
Jack's fat cat looks out.

It's dark.
It's late.
It's raining. It is raining hard.

6

"Woof, woof!" went Spot.

Jack's fat cat likes Spot.
She likes Spot a lot.
Spot needs help.
She runs to help Spot.

It's very dark.
It's very late.
It's raining very hard,
but Spot runs and runs.

Spot runs and runs.
The fat cat runs and runs.
On and on they run.

It's very dark.
It's very late.
Now it is raining very, very hard!
"Hoot, hoot!" went the owl.

On and on they run to the stream.
Spot stops. Spot looks.

The fat cat stops and looks.
The little dog wags his tail.

The moon comes out.
In the stream is a big black log.
On the big black log
they can just see...

11

... three little kittens!

On the log are three little kittens,
three very cold,
three very wet little kittens!

12

Splash!

Into the stream jumps Spot.

He swims and he swims and
he swims to the first little kitten.
He swims back to the fat cat.

13

Splash! Into the stream jumps Spot.
He swims and he swims and
he swims to the second little kitten.
He swims back to the fat cat.

Splash! Into the stream jumps Spot.
He swims and he swims and
he swims to the third little kitten.
He swims back to the fat cat.

Jack's fat cat purrs.
She licks the three little kittens.

Spot is very wet and very cold,
but he is pleased!
He is very pleased.

The fat cat licks
the three cold little kittens.
"Meow, meow, meow!"

Spot licks and licks and licks!
"Meow, meow, meow!"
They are very cold.
The three little kittens
are very cold.

"Help!" yelled Jack.
"Kittens! Three cold, wet kittens in my bed!"

But Jack is pleased.
He is very pleased!

# We hate clowns

"I'm fed up," said Pen.
"I'm fed up," said Pip.
"We are fed up too," said the boys.
"Let's go for a ride on our bikes," said Rob.

"Look," said Ali, "it's a fair."
"Yes. Let's go to the fair.
 It's fun at the fair," said Pen.

"Let's go in the clowns' tent,"
said Pen. "I like the clowns."
"We hate clowns," said the boys.

"Clowns are silly," said Ali.
"Well we like clowns,"
said Pen and Pip and Sue.
"Clowns are funny, not silly!"

"Let's go on the big dipper,"
said Tim.

But the big dipper cost too much.

"Let's go on the big slide," said Kim.
But the big slide cost too much.

"Let's go on the big wheel," said Ali.
"We can all go on that."
"Yes, let's all go on the big wheel," they said. "It is better than the big dipper and the big slide."

"Hold on! Hold on!" said the man.

Up, up, up it went and
down, down, down it went.
Up, up, up and down, down, down.
Round and round, round and round.

Up and down, round and round! Bang!

We are stuck!

I don't like it!

Help! Get us down!

Hold on! Hold on!

Pen!

Pip!

Sue!

"Help! Help!" shouted the boys.
"We are stuck. We don't like it!
Get help! Please get help.
Please get us down,"
shouted Ali.

"I'll get help!" shouted Pen.
"I'll get help!"

"Yes, we can help," said Charlie.
"We can get the boys down."

"Sit still, hold on,
and don't go away!"
said Charlie with a grin.

"Thank you Charlie, and thank you Chump and Munch!" said the boys.

"Let's go in the clowns' tent," said Rob.
"Yes, let's," said Ali.

"I like clowns," said Kim.
"I like clowns very much," said Tim.
Pen and Pip and Sue just grinned!